UTOPIAN RACE

UTOPIAN RACE

Frank Karan

Library of Congress Control Number:		2019900501
ISBN:	Hardcover	978-1-7960-0009-2
	Softcover	978-1-7960-0008-5
	eBook	978-1-7960-0007-8

Print information available on the last page.

Rev. date: 01/15/2019

To order additional copies of this book, contact:
Xlibris
1-800-455-039
www.Xlibris.com.au
Orders@Xlibris.com.au
753778

CONTENTS

ABSTRACT WEALTH

You're mind is frozen in the headlights
Of antiquity whilst downplaying squally
Expletives of dastardly bequeathed kings
In rangy n'gaut brews of stylish fashion

Why don't you roll onto my back? Before
You hit the rough sack, with your mingy
Whiskers softly nibbling my skin like a
Finch in a branch your italicized title

Is inebriatedly calloused like massive
Engraving on some new huge corporation
You can also regain your life carefree
Then you won't mind the monitoring fee

When your served large unctuous rhetoric
You need to take a precautionary measure
Before protruding into the foray mint of
Strategic treasure, you may become a new

Recipient for interoperability's leisure
When you can decertify your notably lame
Insulating quivering self; telegenically
Emanating continency for abstract wealth

ACCUMULATING TOXINS

There are huge restoration procedures that have
To be strenously put into the commonplace those
Allergic swelling complications that lye dismally dormant

Hidden in damp darkened enclosures which are just
As welcoming as uninvited guests an hideous pests
It's freakingly unimaginable to step out from the
Carbon monoxide vat, into a hydrogen sulphide mat

Without fiercely resuscitating the panty hose cat
Is there an emergency antiseptic soothing panacea
To infiltrate the fearsomely aching dizzy spasms
Circulating within the cuts n'bacteria abrasions

Penetrating in your puffed up bleeding wounds
Which are accumulating toxins, thus poisoning
Conveniently your antivenene cluster cul-de-sac
I'm not a preliminary herpetologist or a bionic

Genetic biologist or a much desired toxicologist
The elusive cure is akin to a caring herbologist
Who is crevice leaping whilst you're softly sleeping
Can you carefully avoid, the pent up costly weeping?

ACRID STAIN

I feel like a spindly little kid
Trying to maintain my composure
I'm not in need of disclosure
And rather frightened of exposure

My heart stumps in fertile shame
But to have and to hold you i must
Loudly screech with considerable pain
There's no immunity from your acrid stain

The arable shrub impedes with torrential rain
Undoubtedly blowing up my aura to smithereens
Forcing our muggy dreams. Where is all of the
Conclamation from the cocktail of frustration

ACTIVELY ENCAMPETH

Disoriently, you try to actively encampeth love
Of erudite insolent style, capriciously there's
An insimated atonement foreshadowing a baffling
Insiccation, formidably benighted n'unserveable

Flirtatiously gloating in grievous retribution
It's forebearance is trustingly unfaltering on
Inanimate pestilence lies unshadowed cessation
The prospect of indiscretion is affably diverse

Indefinably n'chattingly in verse. How often do
We sit in strained silence; feigning gaudily in
A scrupulous pandemic curse? Furtively impinging
On a mascaraed lashes, deprecating life's clashes!

ALTRUISTIC APTITUDE

I'm sick n'tired of pampering your spongy demented
Ego and eloquently chuckling the uninviting gazebo
You're conscious ephemerally dangles our languid form
I must try to irrevocably avoid the illimitable storm

There is a much impetus in our do good impulsive impostor
He's belligerently suppliant to a laudable expedition
Does he concomitantly inveterate into another perdition
An epagogue construes, a chuffling equitable fruition

The attitude barrier flows so abhorrently bacchanal
Aggrandizing such unpreventable altruistic aptitude
We listen to the confab within a tocsin cortile advice
Diagnosing sostenuto toccata of an intransitive device

ANDROGYNOUS FLAIR

How many unprintable lines can i read?
To break the road blocking gridlock of
You're hoodwinking alibis? Achingly so
Moronic the fitting room slides; there

Is a desperecy of periphery schnoozing
Hysterically wild, with puffed up lips
And silver tips animatedly chirpy but
Undeniably quirky; shamelessly smurky

You're apartment style glare has got
Androgynous flair with an undeniably
Saucy stare; the up market exclusivity
Is snoggingly surmising it's captivity

ANICONIC AMULET

The enchantress was chanelling in a trance
Opaque was her cloak n'dagger stance, then
Upon her piggyback i'd like to tricky dance
Savagely forewarned, by teleology oblivious

To theology; her encloring temple has somewhat
Disintegrated into tumbledown phut! Truncating
The trepan preciosity of presage, the aniconic
Amulet lacks rogation, cowering in trepidation

ARRANT ARTIFACTS

I don't seek to analyze or cannibalize your situation
It's like a fiscal firth ready to mysteriously birth
Across the board you annul; all the antecedent worth
You're so anthropomorphic and artificially articulate

The arrant artifacts have compatriot concubine defects
Inculcating the arcadia applique; canoodling technique
The colloquial chinstrap implies misogynistic values
Incriminating an incurious incrustation of box n'lox

There's a closed book in your shell shocked vicissitudes
Should we be indebted to the tiniest braggart equanimity
Or the aching wag bowdlerizing cantata of mass proximity
There's a moreish taste in the slap up hot meal delivery

AWKWARDLY REMINISCE

I awkwardly reminisce of that secluded
Backbeach where we met hugged n'kissed
There was little there but the sludgy neap tide
And the elusive pink tailed, feathered cockatoo

Scuttling the gentle silence flying from tree to me
A cataract plunging down upon swimming anchovy fish
The graphic picturesque lagoon with softly sullying
Waterfalls, splattering exotic fauna, towering over

The steamy humid, mid summer's sauna, boiling heat
How could we reflect so visually for the rest of the
Busy turnstile world to see? There's not a singleplace
That I'd rather be, than sharing this moment of you n'me

BARBARIAN BLADE

Yield a blade and break a bone
Mighty warrior's i have known
Torment in life you're not alone
Mysticism belongs to the unknown

My body wanders sacredly alone
Into the magic forest i roam

In search of flesh and bone
Barbarian blade i must own

I can hear the devil's
Treacherous laugh, and the
Hounds of Hell ferocious bark
Adjudicating in contractual dark

The bleak valleys of old unleash
They're vile obnoxious dreadful toll
The voracious fear, repulses my soul
Our life is written like an ancient scroll

BARELY A MURMUR

The aphrodisiac that you opted to give me
Scarcely soiled my crumpy dry barren lips
As you deployed some fragile preaching of
An adventurous conquering tall naval trip

A bootful of rauncheously, chaffed lies
Is impeccably slick, which more or less
Accomplishes the feebly shuffling trick
There's barely a murmur inside a brick!

A merchant ship on rough tide can sink
Then love lights up like a silver chip
Life rapidly becomes a far flung strip
There's barely a murmur inside a brick

BECOME A PAIR

You have to have a fast furious pace
Just to be in the Grand Prix race
Where there is no sorry disgrace
Just actual accelerated mace

Though your eyes smile so bright
And make me feel, tenderly right
They disintegrate all of my lies
Then cut me down to slender size

All i really wanted was you
To stick by me and be true
Think of what we share
When we unite, become a pair

BERKELEIAN PLAN

I bonked so exteroceptive in this unenviable protasis
The mephitis was an unwritten epithet of masked death
My old town was bested in the eye of a hurricane storm
It was discomfited n'made unhereditable, that was the

Norm, my world became obliterated as i leapt in discommode
I witnessed newly born babies infanticided n'infantilistic
Hooligans indicted, as the hidrosis bucketed down into my
Incinerating aching body, the rising Fahrenheit bedazzled

And topped the mercury scale, then struck a hideous gale
Which left me with nothing but a spoon in my soiled hand
I'm not a philosopher, just a simple man working hard to
Earn what i can. Is this the all mighty Berkeleian plan?

BREVITY

You're fruity face looks so very sad tonight
Echoing a deflorating brevity upon some dark
Tilting freezing frame; beneath cold brashness
Of a lost soul there is no coincidence or chance

But only a resounding out of time rhythmic dance
Bruiting the cynics quest of an enticing trance
Subhuman is the overall skeptics benign stance
We can flippantly revel at life, with a glance

BRIGHT EBONY

Plundering the bright ebony of your swampy brain
Tethering the unexposed interacting aimless game
The pain is galvanized in a murky tenacious stain
I'm escaping this tense stand off holographic aim

The sideshow freak gambolingly smiles and numbs us
Decorously posing and conspicuously imposing as if
A judicious composition is resolutely decomposing
I still recall the loveliness of your mid morning

Parquet kiss, it's so instrumental what pastiche bliss
The almoner needs to use the ligature toner with a new
Klaxon cellophane honer; you've now learned to panhandle
A genderless donor. How competent is your current owner?

BROODING ASHES

You always pull the blanket
To your side of the bed
And when you miss a meal
You say your not hungry instead

Your fortress is really a glass
House so don't throw any stones
You quirkly hide away like a miserly
Cat that's jumpy n'comes out to play

Then you clean your fingers after
Shaking the strangers greasy hand
Mimmickly your head can expand
Yet the smoke still rises from

The dirty grotty crooked chimney
In the poisonous dust n'charcoal
Brooding ashes serve to remind you
Of your displaced corrugating pace

Strangely correcting the robotic zombie
Diseased filled human embryo cargo race
In a vacuum without a spirit of place
You may try to conceal your plum face

Lightning strikes us so premature n'
It's constantly hard to remain pure
We need to find a cure and like the
Jackal and the wolf, we must endure

BUBBLY VOICE

You can't give up because
You haven't any other choice
I fell asleep with your soft
Sweet chirpy bubbly voice

And when the morning sun
Awakens my dribbly place
I'll meet my future darling
Right between my happy face

Dark shadows keep reflecting
From scented burning candles
Beaming our minds outwards
Into cosmic heavenly space

Your body resembles ice-cream
Enjoyably melting, in the sun
As you eagerly lick your love
Pleasantly having so much fun

BUFFERED IN BLISS

Our galaxy is like a whirlwind rusty nail
Protruding it's solidity through a cosmic
Cyber rail. Should I have to feel so frail?
Travelling carefully on the animosity trail

Is there a deflection for the latest grisly
Chronic projection? I hope it does not have
A contagious connection or a mimic injection
Our thoughts are naturally buffered in bliss

Of when we excitedly touched sweetly cuddled and
Passionately kissed, you're such a lovable twist
That's why i cannot resist, your frolicking laugh
Is like the morning mist cutely buffered in bliss

CALENDARING MOPE

You could not ever patiently wait for me
You only struggled to find yourself free
You're always straddling to go somewhere
But you did not stay and didn't care for

Anyone but your own egotistical self, your
Debt was a logistical milestone in stealth
The things you craved so patingly refused
To quickly eventuate for you to really be

You keep renumerating, then philosophizing
Like a sage but you cannot quell your rage
Life is beckoning much atrocity, at peak
Monumental velocity. I tightly hold onto

The narrow slippery, mountain coiling rope
I'm not a copycat but I'm learning to cope
It's like a scene from a midday soap, this
Empty hollow sensation of calendaring mope

CARTOONISH STRESS

I deluded myself in a cold strange place
Filled with fainting ghosts n'silver ladies
I felt so petrified n'lullified i thought i
Was going to break out with hives or die

A pitiful dark stare besets me as i bite
My stiff upper lip whilst i thrust my hip
Then downing an alcoholic dry martini trip
I'm so sick n'tired of been cooped up against

The wallowing pressing flesh, it's like an elect
Elicited despicable mishmash of cartoonish stress
We consolidate n'adduce the undisclosable infructuous
Initiative by shrugging suspicion; chugging superstition

CAUTIOUSLY CRAVE

We learn more from the things
We do wrong than the things
We do right, we acknowledge
Objection thus fear rejection

Let's insert a healthier injection
It's interesting to observe; serve
Especially in the twisting curve
You cautiously crave for love on

The double wishing to avoid trouble
I'm not going to do anything bad to
You; I just seek to share quality time
With you. Do you sense stormy weather?

As you unwittingly put 2 n' 2, together
The beginning was connected to the end
Everything was connected to the end
Everything else was trapped in the middle
So why do you continue to play the fiddle

CELESTIAL FRUIT

You jolt so hurriedly like
A rabbit facing headlights
Bopping in silvery shadows
Treading in calfskin boots

Quintessentially fetching celestial
Fruit, misapprehending a marvelous
Connectedness, nattering it's false
Optimism of radiant moonstruck love

You're olive green zephr eyes expose
an eternal warmth n'cyclical mystery
laddened in a golden fabulousness of
almighty dtermination n'abomination

CHINSTRAP OF FRUSTRATION

How can you be bemused in such a concubine
Disoriented state of mind? Your life needs
To be refreshed to unwind, it's like a rare
Precipitated accident or peripheral jerking

Reaction in the absolvent progenitor's time
There's a sense of evil brewing as i try to
Stealthily pull open the loosely long velour
Curtains in your rugged up shabby apartment

Overlooking the terra cota filthy shining city
Whilst sleeping amongst designer, silky sheets
In a shocking regurgitating psychological form
Listening to the unfurling of the leaves croak

Arguing, of freshly wet gutter dancing frogs
A concerning quietness reverberates from the
Chinstrap of frustration, escalating into a
Ventricular fibrillation; What a summation!

CLODHOPPER

You exerted a certain amenity
Posing in a neo classic style
The angosturic ascent undeniably
Ameliorated an unctuous clogmire

Amicably generated a total amiable
Outcome to an insulting clodhopper
He was nothing more than a miserly
Trumped up second rate showstopper

Eftsooning in a morbid sthenic stet, thus
Expropriating the scour sinistral rollick
Expunging between the roguely sinecure of
Alternating throng truism martyr altruism

CONDUCIVE CRESCENDO

We happily sat, ate drank and sang
Shouted slang, extended life's fan
Let me relieve your bitter tension
Seat you in comfortable suspension

Albeit our love of art we traded
Smart departing an splenious mart
With our hearts open to breaches
Appeasing many unexpected niches

To a pleasing conducive crescendo
We stamp out all of the dissonant
Divisiveness, traversing the holistic
Immersion of a patriarchal dispersion

The obelisk pinnacle in obiter dictum
Will seek some valid solution in this
Climatic evolution to avoid the blunt
Infusion of our kaotic mass confusion

CORRALING ANTECHAMBERS

I ignited the passionate fire as you turned
Up the heat, scintillating a monstrous beat
For the sinking Titanic. How could you sell
Life rafts or sophisticated mini submarines
I know you're eager, but still not too keen

The pressing gilt edged tendrils indulge the
Inadvertently debilitating, icy cold fingers
Ensconed in gloomy passageways of corralling
Antechambers within you're repressively static
Inner mind. Is it the message you seek to find

CORRIDORS OF HELL

No one understands the emptiness which I share
It's like the loneliness when you're not there
I'd gladly descend into the darkest abyss lair
To do battle with all the hideous demons there

Through the corridors of Hell I'll bravely dare
And break the treachery of this evil curse bare
Should I have to suffer this indignity without care
My fortitude marches neatly, to the holy drum snare

It's more than a theatre od pain when you violate my
Name; and keep sucking the virgin blood from my vein
There is no pity or shame, in this death defying grave
Yard game! I was just wondering who is there to blame?

COTERIE COUCHETTE

The hectoring wannabes lack the wisdom
Convivial attitude; and warily convoke
Eachother in a transcontinental bustle
Stop tour conically convuscating ampoule
Medicaments of anodyne in a form of well

Emboidened snafu spate; ths consignatorilly
Ccowering n'countervailing a coterie couchette
The geopolitical fulcrum of splash conspectus
Stashing the consortium plate, their contango
Is dirigibly emanciating the judicature state

DEEPER STUPOR

I'm perfectly not convinced with your dodgy
Alibi's and sordid excuses; you're lackluster
Performance reflects your spaghetti thin stamina

You sit sheepishly sucking on morello cherries
Besprinkling your moreish caviar dish, whilst
Waffling over cross refrenced booksy material

The ketamine hierarchy is akin to a mild heparin fixing
Indicative is my discontent in party politics bickering
The indictable fracas has escalated from been incipient

I think I'll just suck upon another sweet hookah
Before i float off and sink into deeper stupor
Sometime later I'll wake up feeling super doper

You're miscreant ego, remains rebatively shallow
It's attached to an incertitude of vain inanition
I'm sure your not planning a wild safari expedition

DOGGEDLY CLOISTERING

The floor needs mopping but your pants keep on dropping
Those fishnet tights expose an erotic phallic intention
Mottle mimicking from the implacable shrubbery tension
I'm gazumped while smooching an still stomach muttering

From the outlandishly funny self mutilating pooching
Puckering up to proclivities and one off festivities
Doggedly cloistering with halfwitted idyllic foistering
The archetypal stylishness is akin, to alien crustiness

The warhorse that you ride, claims a demeaning tide
Life threatening is the scuttlebutt of multivarious
A precarious muddlehut is rezoned as flavoured various
There's water running off the duck's back as we scrape

The sack!

ENFEEBLE RESTIVENESS

You're politicking interference n'abrupt backtracking
Are unspeakably lame, the engrossing demented demands
Opportunistically deployed yet nevertheless enjoyed
An enfeeble restiveness is durably funneled against

Your panicking defences; you cannot jump the fences
Your grandiose lustful eroticism, is capably select
But verifiably incorrect, insufficiently executed is the
Absorption of territorial gains circulating austere pains

FEEBLE UNCERTAINTY

If you can only see my relentless heart
The scenic volcanic eruption inside it
Splatters the exploding molten lava mash
The soaring mercury of whipping hot ash

Is strikingly wild like an eternal pagan bash
With follicles of love i tenderly dare to dash
Into musky luscious mists of feeble uncertainty
Whirling in a steady vacuum of liberating certainty

FUTURE PLANTATION

Why do your answers lack in conviction
Do you service the knowledge addiction
There's more to learning than friction
Where's the authority in your diction?

Expectations fluctuate through our minds
Consequences shut down our silver blinds
Experiences stimulate our sense of reality
Prejudice activates our chance to finality

There's a costly systematic unfolding process
Inviting curiosity and installing information
Sowing the seeds for a vast future plantation
We are our own unique, explicit self creation

Trying to steeve off, the steamroller devastation
Beauty seemingly exists because there is ugliness
Freedom persists; because there is some restraint
Can we create perfection using carbon copy paint?

GIANT WASTELANDS

All feelings are shun when your time is well done
Hidden in a closet whisper, running with the wind
A dampness rises in your avid soul; like arid buds
Blanketed in foliage turning into soft tinted hues

The murky mist seems so inviting thus eager to explore
It's well worth citing where creatures run roam n'soar
Alien shadows walk upon moisty darkened forest grounds
As poltergeist's begin their creepy mischievous rounds

I've yet to taste an inspiration from a tingling spark
Even if it's aromatically fragrant in hibernating bark
There are giant wastelands hidden skywards in my heart
My life has been splattered in sorrowful declivitously

Psycho chemical art; a burning fire licks it's thirsty
Tongue, exhibiting the damage that has been done! Till
The day i die the darkness I've fought and seen. There
Is not an iota of independent interaction to intervene

My fortitude does not possess, a wonderous miracle stroke
Our resplendent dreams divulge a lifechanging winning poke
Shall i take off in a mini moke? Now is not the time to joke
The moon precedes n'recedes. Have you completed your good deeds?

GRANITE FINGERTIPS

Keyboard! The grandeur of splendour, gushes
Profusely from your pale granite fingertips
As you bounce off your ego trips, in the small
Seedy hours there's a genre of belatedly happy

Buzzing hips, impeccable tips, nescience clips
Why should you eat food from contaminated dips
Do you know what you have and what your losing
Don't risk it because it's not worth confusing

GRAVEYARD STREET

My heart fell into the sandpit of discontent
After you kissed me dearly on my perky cheeks
My body mingled to a fantasizingly crispy beat
By our lusty desires we can accomplish any feat

I watch you combing your long, strawberry blond hair
From the emptiness of the chilly cold graveyard street
My soul dichotomizes our love, tiptoeing beneath sparky feet
Your lips are like sugar, flavoured soft n'tantalisingly sweet

HEAL THE WOUND

All the evil dragons have been slain
Now the knights, can be on their way
What adventure lies in store
Will it lead to your front door

Can my love rightfully score
Heal the wound from your paw
Stitch your head above the floor
Strike your heart at it's very core

You throw your smile back at me
As I catch it I'm glad to see
That it's me, and only me
How about some peppermint tea?

Lights are out, they've all gone home
Lights are out, I'm here all alone
It's the dawning of a brand new day
And my love is here to happily stay

We can't have it, any other way!

HIGHER BREED

To live in a fanciful dream is to question why
Anything's possible; even under a fragile sky
The probability of you getting with i is nigh
If you stumble so drowsy then I'll tumble so

Wowsy! There's no time for negligence n'trouble
Let's clear the rubble to overcome the struggle
I wish to go somewhere to watch the snow fall
Far away from the urban sprawl n'cities crawl

Your like a lonely ghost looking for a house to haunt
There's much more to groveling and petty shrovelling
Why don't you look at yourself, straight in the eye?
Do you think you can conceive a higher breed to fly?

HORNSWOGGLE

A horrendous torrent was ensuing when you
Dubiously engorged; the life savings from
Your innocent fellow humanitarian friends
What a hornswoggling feat, full of deceit

I saw a dyslexic tiresome grumpy old man
As he whisked by me glinting his curling
Eyes and guttly spitting from his saliva
Puffing lips, cursing madly he glissaded

Away on thin ice and frosty coloured dirty snow
His odd fricative dull smile became concretised
An emotional disparity garnered in fuming contempt
The unappealing compargation needs austere attempt

There is no citation or highly revered commendation
The peak of perfection has reached fever saturation
The horn pipe won't blow in your favour even though
You're a life saver! Don't worry the insurance firm

Won't settle for a waiver… can you do me favour?

HYPOCHONDRIC LITANY

Your salient efforts immobilizes the flinty
Grubbleness causing bemire shoddy muddleness
There's the inciting texture of unbiddeness
One can only wonder on one's own imagination

Science is vainly in search of a universal
Panacea! Will it cure my ravaged trachea?
It's such a timorous venture, life can be
A tentative adventure, the friar's chimere

Is tainted with saffron tannin's, yet aromatically
Flavoured by essences of veneer, i don't condone
To snoop, in a close knit, tete a tete situation
Maybe you've heard the latest gossip conversation?

You suffer from a lack of suction lipoclastic
And your fonticulus is driving you so spastic
How can we bemoan the formidable iconoclastic
When a hypochondric litany appears so plastic

IMPETUOUSLY FLAKEN

There was a fiery smoke mingling
In the rainy moist windswept air
As the horses hoofs trotted in the
Dusty steamy hot mid morning glare

The boughs and leaves were furiously shaken
My heart and psyche were impetuously flaken
That tuyere scolded my worsted woven jacket
In a blaze of turquoise and reddish bracken

My edgy scone feels like a scapular bone
Is there an esoteric perpendicular zone?
Or a triangulating encyclical car phone
Opprobrious is the extenuating old home

The chessel n'chino are been pecked away
By the frugivorously tame coalmouse bird
Anything else that you've heard is absurd
How can we try to round up the wild hird?

INCESSANT BARRAGE

There was a disturbingly, silent ruckle
After your rumbustious monumental speech
Presented from the chuffed ruins of the
Dilapidated cathedral, i must remind you

That we are not sacrificial lambs even if
We've been conditioned and indoctrinated
With dissertation served in ashen gospel
Peddling the leafy purlins of opprobrium

The alleged coup d'etat is not bound to win
Your rumoured trysts appear anorexically thin
Your lack of motivation is dispensed in the bin
There's no swarthy scowling, or vitriolic howling

You often lack substance and get blown by the wind
Is there a commander to this avant garde conspiracy?
Or a huge betrayal; vindicated in autonomous hostility
I hear a petty utterance off the grotty little boulevard

Countenancing an incessant barrage from the
Astonishingly thrilling 21st century carriage
There are bleaker moments in life than this
Some are unpredictable, but some you can miss

INDISCERNIBLE AXIOM

Do you look up from the tower
Or just assume ultimate power
What do you use to measure success
Is it in recess or a game of chess

Your redolent tears keep shrinking with beers
It's inscrutably haughty and somewhat naughty
This indiscernible axiom highlights your ascension
Thus eloquence is convoluted in a distracting wave

Your dry throat is choking as the concentric rush
Peels away the calumny rejection and ejection that
You make; high stakes and rolling gears play a very
Significant role in all the challenges you must fake

INTERNATIONAL ALLERGY

I'm not affected by the weather, even
Though I'm wearing faded rags n'drabs
There's a monosy of ideas, in lividly
Wandering slow starting rolling gears

What's more bizzare, than ruthless fears
Triumphantly backglancing swotting tears
It's such a complicated, hazardous job
To make the drought even less abhorent

It's nice to push a trickle to a torrent
Like serrated winds upon dolphin fins my
Prodigy is not the biodegradable allergy
The international allergy is the ecology

Been starngualated within biology; clamnishly
Exterminating the zoology, where's our ideology?
There must be a chink in the way our leaders think!
We should be able to manoeuvre their minds not to stink!
We should be able to manoeuvre their minds not to stink

INTRICATELY INTREPID

There was a brattling violation, n'turgid despoliation
Irrepealably apprehensive, mootingly vulgarly wreaking
Irrepressibly haggling, indiscreetly muzzy swaggerling
From the encarcerating derelict diabolic desegregation

The inuvement rectitude is an invariably inutile lift
Attempts to newly amend it are extremely futile swift
Reticent of puerile ambition lathered within the soft
Intaglio of sot smiling lustfully aspiring transition

Seeking the infructuous desiccator n'virily dirigible
Optimistic instigator rehabilitator; your intricately
Intrepid but lack sustenation, the replevin has since
Become redundant, mockery and outrage reign abundant!

INTRUDING INTONATION

There's an intruding intonation stultifying my memory
The internecine coup de tat is exponentially discursive
How can we succumb to the minutely chagrin subversive?
Supervenely chaffing the sinking fund is too suppressive

Sinuously siphoning the setto: abstenously very scantily
It's up to you n'me to up the anty; ablution is so dandy
The invalid moratorium scandalizes itself perfectly handy
It's akin to disembodied candy. So why get so hot n'randy?

IRREGULAR YELPING

Essentially regulating the advancing military
Sealing my fate with a muted heavy kiss while
Besottingly targeting the irregular yelping
There's a soul cleansing freedom disbursing

From the fountains of a scented spring in
Low lying mountains the birdsongs do sing
The raptures overlap, exhausting my scene
I'm not acclimatized with you're buckling

Inarticulate ramblings n' inconsistently soft
Babblings, as we sift through clippings from
The inglenook; a spirketting log fire hungrily
Blazes when you lethargically deny my wages

KINDRED SOUFFLE

There is a soluble intermittent alacrity
Cemented in a burlesqued sostrum society
Divesting the awesomely interrogating criteria
And flagitiously crippling the fiesta hysteria

Emphatically denouncing the hierarchy superior
The deviate lies deliberately bedim sturdy, thus
Fragmentally blethering n' encapsulatingly extorting
Enthrusting a demotic flute cadenza subtlely cohorting

You're fancy linen shirt is in the cabinet calamander
Why try nudging and trudging the inimical salamander?
The nightcap is sparsely bisque, yet there's an elite
Buffet. Would you care for a freshly kindred soufflé?

MENACINGLY UNPERTURBED

Menacingly unperturbed into the clumsical
Realm i scourge; it's bursting to diverge
And unleash what is mine, I run up the cliff
But it's an exhaustively sluggish muddy trip

I'm not on a powertrip but i need to appease
The ancestoral sacrificial gods, they are so
Ferocious, they bite wildly like untamed dogs
I can jump into the volcano boiling with halo

The silhouette mountains keep cropping up in my mind
We'll replace carbon monoxide with dioxide peroxide
Then bring back the missing ageless flora and fauna
Just right around nature's, humanistic earthy corner

MID WESTERN TOWN

You parade around this arid town
Like a sheriff from the old west
Still haunted by ghosts as you dig
Up, dead people's skeletal remains

Your afraid to run into dingy caves
Where sirens cry n' howl over graves
You'll fight tooth n' nail to give up
Any ground, upon this merry go round

You'd get what you ask for, in this
Forgotten dustbowl mid western town
Once glorified, by the nugget pound
A bottle of scotch may put a blotch

In your hungry flee infested bloodhound
You couldn't even catch my handkerchief
As it leapt from my shirt to the ground
A tearful reunion waits in the dogpound

But life n' death go on just the same
Is there anything tame? Only the lame
What happened to the dreams of yesteryear?
Did they vanish, or we're consumed by fear?

MILD MYSTIQUE

Your making me sweat like a long distance runner
But it's worth the wait because you're a stunner
Your face resembles icy snowflakes gently falling
Your pearly hair flows like freshly washed sheets

An your eyes flicker the translucent porcelain treats
Conglobating in a husband serenity of channeling beats
My soul is been soothed by crystal clear calm waters
Lapping at my feet gently i walk upon warm waters of

Pristine yellow sands in a deserted pre historic beach
Whilst lazily sucking, on a refreshingly ripened peach
Sipping pink champagne, tingling with fragrances from
Otago wallflowers scenting their exotic mild mystique

My breath remains google eyed, at the magnificent beauty
Of an orange sunset sky, autumn leaves abundantly rustle
They're sad goodbye; cinnamon n' nutmeg are now in fashion
So why do we have to wait till love becomes fiery passion

MILITATING NATION

Your impish ego imploded into a limberness
Of a fiery implacable gape; you're like a
Stage struck actor whose fumbled his lines
So I'll pull down the dirty curtain blinds

You try to avoid, the circus embarrassment
Are you afraid of the critical harassment
The congruous gargantuan uhlan committed
Tyrannicide ousting of glomerate suicide

The militant's army faces a perilous defeat
It's wiser, to advance backwards in retreat
The imperial king is suffering from neuroma
Thus we bemoan his psychotic neural misnoma

His royal splendor, continuatively quashes
All opposing foes his parados is kept under
Watchful eyes overseeing the passing huanaco
Grazing in the long morass blue stem tobacco

Can tinctures be a source for our salvation?
We don't have to go into reclusive hibernation
Equitation is adhered to like hyper ventilation
Can we liquefy this impromptu militating nation?

MONOLITHIC FOUNTAINS

You stirringly partboil my illicit senses
As you protrude my awesome fetish defences
Your dressed in a twill garbadine sequin mesh
Canvassed on coffee coloured fringed balconies

Drifting my ego monde into a bleak serac
I'm made to feel like a whimpering slave
Dusting off the firecracker brave, knave
As we proceed to make love in the robust

Pompeiian gardens, gilded by monolithic fountains
There's a monitory silence hanging over our heads
Like the merciless impending sword of Damocles
It's life threatening n' not just a mere tease!

Indignantly, I'll retreat back to my cosy skio
Where the continuum is a bohemian tzigane trio
Is there some leeway, to paravane the puzzling
Computer motherboard and monocle chequerboard?

MYSTERIOUS MEETING

There was a mellow time when
The spirits walked the earth
And the new age gave simple birth
Life wasn't made up of mere mirth

You cannot escape the deadly curse
It's like a deadman's filthy purse
Flowered fences accelerate the climb
As spiritual heaven is purely divine

Can you see the elusive bush fairy
Or the magnificent coloured canary
Are you in search of the soul ferry
Or still collecting milk from dairy

You're cloak n' dagger style is
Hidden within a welcoming smile
There's more to give and take in a
Mysterious meeting; where love n' life

Become fleeting, you're flesh is totally
Rotting as your brain is numbly trotting
You're like a hungry wolf forever spotting
So what's to stop the evil, from plotting?

NEOLITHIC BOOM

Perserverance pays dividends as I make no amends
From snowline to sunshine in sheep drought sand
To empty carapaces, lies the fog covered tarmac
Of your cul de sac, never never land, it's not

So counterproductive to now look back and wonder
What did it all mean? Soft khaki leather cradles
My silting aching corns, as I've trodden over
Many sunny pristine thorns, my foot callouses

Are half an inch thick, yet I yearn to frolick on
A sunlit kick, if I move eagerly quick I may pull
A magic trick, as I straddle upon the website of
Your cocoon, beneath the neon holistic half moon

Pouncing under the ultra Neolithic boom, a fresh
Pattering scripture in the medieval, gothic tune
Deforesting the lungs of our entire mother earth
Can we regenerate a timely brand new world birth

NEW AGE SCRUFFIAN

You're lips taste like broken beer glass
As your fingertips tingle like sharp ice
You're footprints puta heavy mark onmy
Downtrodden soul as I sprint like a foul

But what's there to run to? When your so
Freezingly cold! I'm not a strange hairy
Ape ruffian but just a new age scruffian
The high waisted designer belt makes you

Look more curvaceous and slender, than you've
Ever felt, the misty fruity fragrance sprayed
Upon your skin tingles like you've never smelt
Do I need a swipe card to show you how I felt?

NEVER CLEARING MIST

You're breath is like icy snowflakes
Scuttling on my delicate window pane
Gargling in a motion of intermittent
Love drying in a never clearing mist

There is much more which we missed
Consolidating the frustrating fist
Evolving from the ever revolving cist
When in love, should you truly insist

My mind keeps flickering through the
Wonderful memories which we had; and
The memorable ones that we never had
So why does love, have to be so sad?

NO ONE ELSE WILL EVER DO

How are you keeping my midnight darling
Have you amassed much fortune and fame?
Are you still writing you're life long diary
Or are you nibbly pursuing some awesome game

What do I have to say to excite you
What do I have to do to ignite you?
My mind is like a big sharp razor blade when the
Sirens sway: just marvel at the world around you

Look outwards, and it will completely astound you
So how do you expect me to wholeheartedly forget you?
I want you to honestly know that there's no one else but you
I live for you n' only you, because no one else will ever do!

NORIMONO ABIDANCE

Whence chiding the adjuring del credere canonically
The lewd connivance was performed economically lisp
They're emboldened appearance is immaculately natty
The alto gossiping voices were bickering very batty

The Yggdrasil had the emblem of St. Agnus Dei
In a yare abstract way, the will o' the wisp
Displayed it's auriferous; fait accomli form
I was left swooning with the agonic artform

The avaricious cortege shelter's it's needy, greedy reliance
The annotinus becloud exhibits regurgitating, unique defiance
There's a wistful anomaly, fiercely embellishing our alliance
We'll gently absolve and foster the beloved norimono abidance

NOTHING'S IMPOSSIBLE

When my hands were firmly tied
You grabbed the ropes and broke
The knot; then I saw the strong
Power that you begot

You came to my aide as soon
As possible, that's why i
Know that with you, that
Nothing's impossible

ONLY YOU

I've waited so long
To hold you strong
N' whisper in your ear
Every naughty little fear

I often wondered why we
Are kept physically apart
But happily near in heart
I feel your spirit over mine

Now I can calmly recline
And drink my dry red wine
My favourite preoccupation is you
I want you and only you

Spunkily your warming desire
Keeps tinkling hot the fire
Unsplintering my nervous spine, the door
Of the chapel is open wide, the bell rings with a chime

OPAL ORANGE MOON

I'm tap dancing on a hammock in
The Acapulco sun, primping on a
Holiday with lots of saucy fun
Drinking tequila and white rum

Under the festive opal orange moon
Love abounds, swiftly and too soon
This frugal hesitancy, blemishes you're
Iconic vigour thus changing your figure

Just keep on slipping the tasty frumpy liquor
There's a besetment of dovetailing to upcast
Wailing; so don't bury your face in my chest
Because I'm not a lame bird, building a nest

You have such a tongue twister of a name
Which adds mockery to your auspicious claim to fame
Jagged webbing resembles your gastric sunken, soreish eyes
Submerging prosperity in leagues of rubble; we're in trouble

OPPORTUNITY KNOCKS

He lived his dream thence sold his soul
But nothing fulfilled his lifetime goal
He had an ambition laden with suspicion
His plans became unfold, his heart wore

No gold other lips did kiss when his darling hot
Love missed. So why give in to peer group pressure?
When you can ascertain that much desirable pleasure
With uncountable treasure; you can be king for more

Than a day, and have me in my peculiar yet cheerful way
But we must remain careful because all can be taken away
Why think as sly as a fox or jump like a jack in the box
We must always keep vigilant because opportunity knocks!

OUR STAGNATION

Across the wide and stormy Viking sea
Blushingly we'll meet and drink our tea
How many wars have been stupidly started?
How many lives have been miserably departed?

We need to start communicating willingly
And stop going to war so enthusiastically
We must also listen cautiously yet effectively
To air our grieviances prudently n' harmoniously

Like a dratted rabitt, the invading infidels will run
With spontaneity our motivating achievements will hum
You sway in solitude; pitifully fragile is your charm
Like a bewitching nymph in the wood, no one will harm

There must be some correlation to our stagnation?
We're all creatures of creation, and not from some
Outer space alien nation! Does this scenario require
More in depth investigation? Where's my commendation?

OVER YOUR LONGLEG

You pistol whipped my frail heart
As i jolted on the wooden bedpost
From our hotbed over your longleg
My heart always longs for what we

Missed as passionately we kissed
Graciously n' cutely i fantasized
Upon the solitary sea the quotidian
Lure was telepathically endured, in

The contesting dailiness of life, just
Keeping myself out of strife, with the
Pre emptive grimace of scolding tears
We grudgingly harassed breaching fears

PALTRY PINNACLE

There's a tiny cacophony of incivility
Goaded by a rival, fizzy pungent melee
Cogently disbursing the convivial paean
We cannot condone the conjuror's tirade

Or the incubus towards a paltry pinnacle
If there's not enough collyrium for your
Sweaty eyes, you may lapse into delirium
How reticent is your panjandrum grimace?

The augur is accessing the incessantly skiff but
Olifant seizure; which lies inchoately bereft of
Propping up in a mondial cavorting fizzure teaser
There's no clause to impoverish impolitic amnesia

PARDON THE PROFANITY

My bloodshot eyes were filled with tears, as the
Surgeon exsanguinated all of the deceased bodies
The aftermath of the twister hurricane resembled
A war zone: with many buildings destroyed deadly

Death and destruction were bitterly deployed, all of
The flora n' fauna had been, vehemently exterminated!
For many miles around i felt like I'd lost the round
To that miserable extortionate banshee sound, that's

Why i earnestly salvaged whatever i could. As i
Expostulated this unfortunate calamity, even to
The echelons of government and humanity, it's times like
These that you can plead insanity; pardon the profanity!

PARVENU PARRY

You're so unremittingly whimsical that your
Supra orbital winces in a pernicious manner
The perspicacious verjouce sequaciousness which
You sanctimoniously shrive is a pernoctation of

Sundry paternal; lamenting, smattering parables
When you welcome the voluble parvenu parry it's
Embracing the avidly indulging kiss n' tell carry
How many coins can you deposit, for a blind Harry?

Audibly mingling with the intangible cinematic attic
Incrusting from the myriad miscible kinematic static
Have you contracted the selective, mydriastic myotomy?
How is your incrementing minimalistic micro cacophony?

PINNACLE STOIC

The cantilevers in your mind are
Thwart with amplified electricity
As the thurible burns it's incense
With a thermal angelic elasticity!

There's an incertitude, leading to
The pinnacle stoic, incavating your
Soul to the point of mocking heroic
Why indulge so ambiently plethoric?

The squirearchy are slowly stodging you up
Purveying n' surveyinh your profligating pun
The strategist thus spirantly succumbs A-one
Propinquity is interrogated by the kingly sum

PITEOUSLY PLACATE

The ramifications of that ramshackling phantasm
Needs to be rapaciously n' diligently spruced up
The unflinching draconian ratbag keeps otiosely
Overshadowing, the veining photogenic premiere

Phosphorescene, I feel like a fuddy duddy who's
Thrown away his periwig and tight fitting skivvy
My crusty brain keeps perpetrating in a pedantic
Sleuth; our entrepreneur lies flabbergasted with

A congenial fealty, his pitchfork tongue is laden
Pitiably vile, that ogle philandering pip squeak
Sits on dusty pincushions staring piteously placate
The tartar old boy network wears a tarpaulin jacket

And pince-nez glasses, pinching with a slight pique
Exuding pizazz, such melodrama peels a powder flake
They enthusiastically eat life like a doughnut cake
Carte blanche is they're bipartisan unfettered cape

PLEASINGLY ZAPPED

We made love in every open special solemn way
As the clouds overlapped, I scrambled for your
Hand, so lovingly you slapped my sweating face
Tingling with sincerity rejuvenating integrity

Your pretty love wings have often been flapped
As my lonely virgin heart is zealously trapped
This amorous sensation is refreshingly capped
The titillating senses, are pleasingly zapped

Stop whining! We're due for some fine dining
Even though our nervous lives, are colliding
I wish to lye in a box of fluffy duck pillows
To glisten above the daydream rainbow willows

I've journeyed past the backbone of your soul
Defragmenting the particles in the black hole
I've now got nothing else left that is of old
Can you barter with something when it's sold?

POIGNANT ACRIMONY

Amongst the muddy bushrock, a pretty little angel
Silently weeps, as I walk alone the forest creeps
The incendiary culprit is not some famous celluloid hero
His achievements amount to nothing more than simply zero

This parasite is so cunning n' furiously running
With poignant acrimony there is something phony
From one fatality to another, it's the antecedent
Inquietude; and primeval insensate moral attitude

A cannibalistic fortitude ingurgitates the steadfast
Plural recalcitrant bravado; begrudging his affluent
Appeal and min linear zeal, his persona non grata within
Rearguard strata is an example taken from his alma mater

PROCURABLE CURRENT

Your unquenchable thirst initiates
A procurable current, vindicating
The procumbent fugitive inside of
My tussive id; unwittingly you hid

My head feels like it's been rammed
Into a wrestling turnbuckle, inanely i
Violently chuckle, umbilically sneezing
In a cogwheel of mediocre unavailing twerp

Exists a tutelary of encumbering nebulous
In the far reaches of your revenging mind
Expunging and proselytizing the exurbing
Regions of your post meretricious novels

Your deeds are purple heart commendable
As the profits soar so prudently bankable
I'm sure your staff is above board amendable
Is there a safety net for been held culpable?

PROLONGED WEIGHTLESSNESS

Have you heard the sound of the calming
Ocean inside the shell? Or the fluently
Tossing of the seawater rolling endlessly
Bridging the illustrious rainbow nightsky

The washing of the neap tides and the
Pendulum crashing waves; we no longer
Live life in caves, there us a spirit of
Adventure spuning the windwarding shores

Our ships are running from pirating coves
Sometimes one's destiny has to be altered
Because lives can be adversely faltered
Reefing the topsail in a Marconi rigged

Jibstay, the emptying ballast tanks pose
A questionable outcome: towards the vast
Seaspraying humdrum, stevedores tie the
Anchor's rope to the capstan, then I'll

Return to voyage the treacherous sea as an admiral
Chieftain! A good teacher evaluates what he teaches
A devout holy preacher enlightens us when he preaches
There's a prolonged weightlessness, as gravity reaches

PUNCTURED FAULTNESS

You've been scampering over the campus station
Bypassing a subfuse of unattendant disclination
Festering the disincentive stupendous acclamation
You're deputation has some detracting appreciation

Savoir fair is as remote as the Alaskan bear
Derivably subjugating, departively deceivious
And spiflicated in the realms of the delirious
The sloven flavor lies unerringly disingenuous

There's nothing amicable in your anabatic ambush
Maddeningly, we stumble through meagre blindness
Unvelentingly escaping a sourly punctured faultness
Defribulising the swollen toothache, of squalorness

PUSSY CAT CHARM

Let's not start a debate
Then end up in hate
Don't put me on hold
And get knocked out cold

It's the law of the land
To pay tax on demand
Stop your timid barking
And pay for the parking

Communication breakdown takes two
Appreciation gladly moves us thru
My only thought was of sweet you
Giving me love like I never knew

Wholeheartedly all I ever wanted was to
Snuggle up to your cute pussy cat charm
And offer you a resting place under my arm
In my lovable way I'd keep you out of harm

REBUT THE SPEAR

A calming gesture draws me near
Hold my hand, dispense the fear
Dust away the cold remnant tear
Ingesting truth n' nothing queer

Love is the token held very dear
It's intangible; rebut the spear
Is the future only for the seer?
I'll put forth my highrise gear!

Tell me the reason why I just
Keep going till the day I die
Ccan you give me strong wings
When it's time for me to fly

RECONNECTING IDEA

You're untapped resources lies slightly peppered
With ambition, dispelling the cynical tradition
Notching up a derided blokey posture be careful
You don't absorb the left over sulking moisture

The office cloud bank is uncertainly flailing
Diminishing returns are preeminently sailing
It's sircumventing a somnambulistic wailing
We can't accept rudimentary preconceptions

Of half witted omnivorously clumsy projections
There's a minuscule receptocal scrutinizing us
Pending upon our multifaceted reconnection idea
How do we separate the limenent, from our peer?

RECUMBENT TRICKERY

Your persona ingrata hails from a hailstorm
Familiar strata, coarsening the wavelength
Of the egregious, famulus n' exotic stimulus
A widespread substitute is the phraseology

There's no disguising insincerity or issuing
Recumbent trickery, dispassionately invoking
The intermediary of reassurance, the undesirable
Perpetrators are indefensibly attuned, anodizing

Their pungent spoon, helplessly buccaneering then
Carelessly purse raking encountering life taking
Whilw stretching the bounds of reciprocal brawling
There's no reconnaissance to contemptible crawling

This is surely the unpredictable mercantile game
Where every supplier n' consumer has only to gain
Diligence is imperative in modest altered states
We can find the adventure if I open up the gates

RESPERSIVE ID

It's like exenterating some respersive id
Consecrating a dilemma within assuage lid
The lack of initiative is highly resoluble
And manipulated by fate; but not by chance

The ground rules are set with exercitation norm
Performing in a rather passive vulnerability of
Unflagging assuetude, the preamble resipiscence
Introduces a plethora of knowledge, seldom seen
And shares itself to those who are all too keen

RUTTED GLORY

You've smudged you're whole life's story
By a perfunctory of grossly rutted glory
Spitting your ugly pernicious words so very
Discardingly causing a frenetic resurfacing

Upon my abandoned, battered virginal soul
How did you abernate from the whole truth
Why did you become so utterly hypocritical
Abrogating in some melancholic sybaritical

Aggravating the hibernating upper echelons
Transducing in pithy miniature pentathlons
What garrison's shall you deploy?
To take siege, of Einstein's toy!

SAFEGUARD MOMENT

There is so much more, I could have said
To you in that safeguarded moment albeit
Which abreaction was abbreviated as I coldly
Sussed out your sycophantic manic expression

Devoid of any form of unreasonable depression
Lying on your newly bought studio suede couch
You were snuggly reading the latest paperback
Thriller, such suspense in a chiller then you

Displeasingly tossed out, last year's hardback
Sealer; there's only a peripheral advantage to
Gain as I set out from the port of call in shame
Abjunctive is my fame, I cannot abdicate my name

SHIELDED CEASEFIRE

The communique from a shielded ceasefire is not
Forcibly heard, respect isn't amicably incurred
With unusual chicanery we observe the emotional
Glinting gallery; Where's all of the normality?

You're merchandising schedule is whimsically fuming
The acrid glittery rigmarole, is bitterly consuming
I turn a blind eye to your silly outburst of innane
Laughter, because they're hamstrung with my plaster

You can't satisfy the thirst with a knee deep burst
It's merely a diversion to the old mendacious purse
Which vulgar underbelly is still squabbling outside
Regathering n' wallowing to the grandiose mediocrity

SORELY BLED

Thank you very much, for your magic touch
You look so delectable n' super acceptable
You're beauty astounds n' profounds. Many men
Will come from all races, and far off places

In childhood I was always cradle fed as i
Appeared almost dead; I often laid in bed
The escapades of King Henry I quirkly read
Now I'm weak n' sore, I can't give you more

My body sorely bled and many tears did I shed
I couldn't even keep myself awake or well fed
It makes me spastic, that you're so fantastic
I want to jump on your box n' rewind the stiff

Rotating clocks. How can that be a selfish paradox
Just stop the prognosis and prescribe proper doses
I'm like a wound up cobra aiming not to miss your kiss
Exotic juicy fruits have flavor as my love did savour

SOVEREIGN CITATION

The quiescent dilettante dissertation was procuring
A nomadic life, procrastinating in an onstinate but
Ostentatious superficial whickering Nietzche strike
Just like a musketeer; ruefully running along musky

Moors. Trying to supplicate the ruley parapet laws
In between the musty megalith he amusingly ponders
Life is like a mizzly mediator permeating a whinny
Disconsolate negotiator and superficial terminator

Often nurturing a preemptive mollifying instigator
Can we supplant the shrewdly vicarious tax collector
Vexing the parvanimiously repugnant of sovereign citation?

SPANGLED CAVE

The hungry dogs of war show duty devotion
So what's with all the mixed up commotion
Whipped up in a frenzy of cynical emotion
Evulgating the creaky, scenario explosion

The archenemy elopes in a stylish scandal
Squirming in a moody pusillanimous handle
Emanciating it's exiguously scenescent candle
Ebbing at the lowlife profiteering scoundrel

Our allegiance is piddling like an erostrate
Ballooning architrave, mimicking you're shy
Sullen voice softly singing in the cold grave
A holy light twitches, from the spangled cave

STOPPED TRYING

This parsimoniously splendid combination keeps on
Featuring so unduly in a captively held situation
Partitioning the parturient labours of alchemic love
There's an industrious signatory, unwilling to shove

Wouldn't the world be such a happy, wonderful place
If we could all live together with a loving embrace
But we've betrayed our planet, and now it's dieing
Did we give up the will, or simply stopped trying?

SULCATING STRATH

The stevengraph simplifies stipple frame
Poised in a scenario of sulcating strath
It's more luxurious than a sulphuric tub
The eidolon swishes the trolling eidetic

Surceasing the prolific stertoric manner
The truism trundles over storiated piles
Speechifying into a voluble affirmage in
The retinue of vast podgy looking people

Displaying a caricature n' portraiture in
Squabbly scribbling and satchel nimbling
Scuffing with grotesque staccato pitched
By our sibling of covetous rookie bravado

TALL TATTLE

The stringendo passacaglia, evoked an intercession
In our inveterate reciprocating dazed relationship
As the catalyst was a cocktail of rich tall tattle
An invidious actuary performed his frugal facility

Stashed in a catallactic timocratic vair formality
Solicitously attesting to the autistic smithereen
Our knockout knighterrant was inviolably pursued
As a limp wristed toughnut new centurion linchpin

Knackered by years of weary kleptomanian battle
A kingly sum bestowed in the archipelago chattel
The anoxia aurora illuminates the mattamore castle
As anosmic polychrony reflects a soothfasting hustle

TEMPORARY TREPIDATION

I'm such a sad excuse for the entire human race
I can't recall where I've been or who I've seen
My parents say I'm lazy and people think I'm crazy
That's why I need a wake up smash in the face call

What a degenerate perplexing situation? A no win
Cul de sac abrasion, wrapped up in a defgramenting
Meager pathetic installation; I feel like I'm under
Some unprescribed neurotic medical sedation elation

Where's the salvation? That's why I'm opting for freeing
Liberation, to give me sound levelling approximation, so
Whimsically decumbent; there's a single solution to deviate from
The temporary trepidation, of manifesting confusion, in illusion

TOTEMIC

Whilst climbing the peaks of the high Rockies
The chinook revitalized my hungry torpid body
As the egregious chippy state scattered away
The awesome crystal blue sky sparked in the

Chink trichroic stages, lamenting a chilling
Fugue of troat, harnessed in umble chiliad's
Trite is the cool of this morning roving land
A chrysalis lies eerie, within the chinidoxa

Whilst we expurgate a rutilant, stigma boxer
In landscape artwork our mountains appear as
Artificial paperweight, in reality they seize
Upon unsuspecting freight, we can't impede by

Chrominance; as nature ploughs it's dominance
The earth loving magic fearing ancient Indian
Tribes were fiercely totemic, as we now walk in
Their history's footsteps and listen so polemic

TWISTED SHAME

As you conceitedly grin at me with cheek
I pistol whip my tongue; clench my teeth
You're the consummate woman riding high
Upon a sensuous aphrodisiac surfing wave

There's a brief conclamation, processing
A splendid effigy of petty twisted shame
Running coarsely, in your battered frame
Thus recanting your once worshipped name

The pillar of society, caught up in a game
With a litany of bad lies are we to blame?
Bombarding our perceptions, no one is sane
How can you escape this recalcitrate pain?

To win or lose is not the entire aim
There's nothing much left to reclaim
Only a minimal amount of sad disdain
Can I cut out some of the mad shame?

UNREMITTING CHIME

Methodically you raise, contentious alarmism
Cruelly scaremongering the unremitting chime
All predictability is conceitedly obliterated
Infimitesimally trekking a sour pumpkin patch

In you're middle aged stalwart sluggish mind
What source supplies the syllable minstrel to
His respectively discordant unmelodious tune
Maybe he can bury his head in a desert dune?

UNQUESTIONABLE IMAGINATION

The muddy ground is fuming, the riverbed is dry
The fruity smell of mangoes scent the tropical sky
The redback spider weaves it's web, no time to cry
On top of the mountain ridges we'll watch the world die

How does one peer down upon man's devastation?
Is our planet doomed or in need of vilification
Shall we avoid this star spangling gratification
Can we look forward to some soothing intervention

How stretched is you're unquestionable imagination?
Imprisoned in a whirlwind of divine manifestation
Dark winds are whistling on our opaque destination
What inconsistency is immersed in this falsification?

UTOPIAN RACE

You kept on saying that
You wanted me someway
You kept on saying that
You wanted me someday

My intenstines rode n' erode
Pulse knitted, then explode
How can we swim in blood
Infested with HIV up above

My thoughts enclosed as the
Spirits proposed; acid rain
Greenhouse pain; humanity's vain
Please put me on the right plane

That's why I wish, we all could
Live in a peaceful, perfect world
Where everyone has no reason to
Feel threatened or sad. We should

All be able to live even with
Out faults and be completely
Forgiven n' understood as we
Emabark upon a utopian race

Harnessed without skepticism
Confusion, ridicule and hate
With a melodramatic soaring pace
Rallying together, to become ace

We can live and learn from
Our resourceful animal friends
Adopting methods to make amends
And save the world before it ends

No one will ever feel out of
Place, or fall from grace
Once we have developed
The utopian race

WALLOWING VAPOURS

You're wallowing vapours are now embalmed
In my battle torn, bloody bequeathed skin
Unnerving the pandemonium of banishment
Within the incomparable unnigard malice

There's a unilateral legacy for equatorial formations
From the ice region glaciers to tropical destinations
You look like you've fallen into a dirty black trench
Your ineptitude has uncovered a crystalline old bench

The tornado is angrily whirling, shockingly twirling
Where moments away, from nature's impending whirring
A distinct luminous replica begins to vaguely appear
Pushing my spirit beyond the higher leviathan sphere

Mildly, there's a message yet so clear
Can I swear an oath to keep you near?
I'll give my life, for you my dear!
Is everything enough, or do you still fear?

WE CAN ENJOY

I want to share my dreams
And ambitions with you
I want to share my fears
And frustrations with you

I wish to seek out all
My passions with you
I wish to seek out all
My fashions with you

We can enjoy lovemaking!
Just like hot bread baking
We can melt the arctic ice
With fire n' sizzling spice

We can have many little things
That are nice and will suffice
I'll cherish you till the day I die
But for now, it's time to say goodbye

WHAT HAPPENED TO WOODSTOCK

I don't have much money
And I don't really care
To support a system that's
False and not totally fair

I'm going to turn my back on all
The lies and unrealistic expectations
Illusion's confusion's blocking out my brain
With some pent up heavy handed patronizing vile

Whatever happened to Woodstock?
Over half a million rolled up there
Chanting for freedom, peace and love
A nuclear free planet n' some clean fresh air

What we've got to do now
Is paint a brand new picture
Of love and sharing in order to
Abolish the clutches of poverty's snaring

Whatever happened to Woodstock?
Over half a million rolled up there
Chanting for freedom, peace and love
A nuclear free planet n' some clean fresh air

WHIRLPOOL IN YOUR PANTS

I don't seek to plagiarise your ideas
Or minimize your casual bohemian life
I won't wish to diffuse your angst
Or cause a whirlpool in your pants

Anyhow, we can crawl around like ants
I never got to kiss the sweetest lips
In town, because you were always too
Unique to consider and have me about

I may not be the greatest guy that has ever been
But you have never ever witnessed what I've seen
As I watch the three quarter moon turning full
I can imagine feeding you by the swimming pool

WISTFULLY MOPING

I'm wistfully moping at the delicately
Moondrenched skies unreliably spraying
Their contingent of asteroids n' comets n
Space junk vomits, a component of cosmic

Mystery is compelling our scepticals minds
There's a margin of transfer n' withdrawal
And of insufficient consultative measures
Stabbing at my poorly comprehending brain

Is our primitive knowledge scattered in vain?
Do we lack the disbursement of disclosing any
Permanent gain? Can we facilitate an enviable
Advantage, regardless from the cost and pain?